Nature is Everything

SEEDS OF WISDOM FOR THE MATURING INTELLECT – BOOK TWO

By Nelunika Gunawardena Rajapakse

Copyright

Philosophical Wisdom

Rooted in LOVE

In homage to my parents
Dionicious and Mildred Gunawardena

Let us sow the seeds of culture
In our children's hearts from the very beginning

So that they may grow to love, to wonder, and to marvel
At the ever unfolding story—the wisdom of humanity

Let their love be unconditional
So it may permeate the world in its totality

Let us inspire our children to understand, and to cherish
The deeper meaning of their love
For they are the keepers of social integrity

Let us, hence, nourish their intellects
With unbounded opportunity

To appreciate the interdependent realities…
The expressions of the human spirit

Which leave behind their everlasting imprints
Called, culture and diversity

Nelunika Gunawardena Rajapakse

Dedication

This is a Special Tribute

In Reverence to My Beloved Parents

Dionicious and Mildred Gunawardena

who lived to epitomize

the wisdom of loving kindness and compassion

towards all beings and forms

who traversed their paths on Earth,

throughout their lifetimes.

Foreword

This book is a 'Seeds of Wisdom for The Maturing Intellect' presentation— Book 2—for the children of humanity, aged six years and above, who deserve to be immersed with knowledge at the base of TRUTH. Our temporal experience is the product of sensory impressions and associated emotive and cognitive thought processes. However, when a child matures with intellectual curiosity and imaginative reasoning, grounded upon his experiential journey of life, it is time that his human tendencies—marked with unique individual sensitivities—are matched with phase and time appropriate opportunity, to penetrate the depths of knowledge.

To nurture the nature of a child, succinctly said, is to support him in light of his unique psychophysical characteristics—in adherence to his particular developmental phase.

There are four formative developmental periods, though, to keep in mind. These range from conception through twenty-four years of age.

The following is an outline of the transformational phases of human metamorphic development—from childhood to adulthood:

- The most impressionable, tender being of 0—6 years

- The maturing personality of 6—12 years (endowed with a curious imagination and a reasoning intellect yearning to understand his world)

- The adolescent of 12—18 years (a sensitive and vulnerable worldling in formation and transformation under the influence of active hormones)

- The young adult of 18—24 years (aspiring to stabilize his twofold human purpose—for his own sake, and for the world at large)

In consideration of the fact that a maturing personality of six years and above is a curious explorer of his greater world—the infinite universe, the more he grows to understand Nature's inner workings, the more passionate he may become about LIFE.

Foreword continued

The happy consequence of nurturing the human body, mind (intellect), and spirit—phase appropriately—is to witness a fulfilled, maturing personality imbued with a wholesome outlook on life. He will cherish each breath of his human condition with appreciation and admiration, wonder and awe, and finally, gratitude for all that is—realizing that he is an integral microcosmic aspect of the macrocosmic whole, receiving from, and returning LOVE with reciprocity to the universe.

As you may note, the content of this book calls for investigative and reflective attention. The propitious transmission of seeds of knowledge, while there is demonstrated readiness to embrace information, is the key point to make.

Therefore, pointers to in-depth understanding, exploration, and discovery of life in the universe must take place in the form of **an unfolding story of LIFE;** it must begin from a discernible point in history. Along this process of discovery—as to who we are, and what we are—by means of this beautiful unfolding story of LIFE, the very experience of 'living to learn' or 'learning to live' must be grounded upon the base or bedrock of morality, as the compassionate, underpinning wisdom of the universe.

Differently expressed, the nature of our universe at its core, or ground, epitomizes the ultimate wisdom or TRUTH in action—as compassionate healing of the highest order; it upholds the principles of EQUALITY and RECIPROCITY in consideration of all beings and forms that wish for their happiness. The manifest universe becomes a field of eternal redemption—placing moral responsibility upon the exercise of FREEDOM—in response to the actions of human FREE WILL.

This is where the story must begin; the fusion of the four wondrous energies of resistance, cohesion, motion, and transmutation interactively bring forth all magical sensory phenomena that we—as terrestrial beings or forms—experience in terms of the substances, in the luminous emptiness of SPACE.

'Nature is Everything'—'Seeds of Wisdom for the Maturing Intellect'—Book 2, is an enlivening presentation of our sensory world of phenomena. Our sentient configuration, in whatever form it may take, is the very consequence of a collaborative union; it is based upon the relation and combination of substances—inorganic matter, in the form of emergent physical frameworks governed by the conditioned interactions of elemental substances, and organic matter, in view of life-elements subjected to processes of natural selection. Thus, our sensory body—along with associated sensory-events—is none other than the product of interplay between its reflective elements (of subjective sense-bases) and the projective elements (of objective sense-stimuli), in terms of Nature's substances that pertain to the relative dimension of 'life and being'.

However, it must be emphasized that the substratum underlying the existence of all spatial bodies of relativity is the primordial essence of LOVE.

This book, in particular, intends to elucidate the unfolding story of LIFE—in its magnanimous splendor—from brilliance to darkness. Every phenomenon—from the infinitesimal to the infinite—is the very unobstructed interpenetration and engagement of all phenomena. We call this the universe of implicate order!

In addition, it is a profound telling of the advent of man empowered with the potential to surpass his innate instinctual tendencies. Yes, this unique being, endowed with an upright and adaptable physique along with a psyche powered by volition, reason, and imagination, is looked upon as the determinant of unfolding human time operating in tandem with nature's sublime <u>moral</u> principles of 'equality and reciprocity'.

All in all, it is my fervent hope that this book, upon your reading and its completion, will arouse deeper curiosity, appreciation, and admiration for all that we experience as the wondrous nature of LIFE!

Table of Contents

The GREAT SELF of LOVE

Photo Credit to: Heather De Grandis

Appreciating the Magnanimous Wonder of LOVE and Its Attributes!

Characteristics:

Essence Body of Infinite Potential that Manifests Ceaseless Phenomena in All-Permeating Space through the Union of Four Material Energies: Resistance (Solidity), Cohesion (Fluidity/Humidity/Moisture), Transmutation (Warmth), and Motion (Motility)

LOVE, All Over!
1

I am 'essence primordial'—through infinite time.

I am 'LOVE inconceivable'—through infinite time.

I am 'the five energies, wondrous'—through infinite time.

I am 'earth, water, fire, air, and spaciousness'—through infinite time.

I am 'space, the womb of all phenomena'—through infinite time.

I am 'playful wakefulness'—through infinite time.

I am 'presence alive'—through infinite time.

I am 'the source and culmination of all events'—called LIFE—as 'empty essence', through infinite time!

LOVE, Selfless and All-Permeating
2

I am **'stillness, in dynamism'**—through infinite time.

I am 'acceptance without expectation'—through infinite time.

I am **'dynamism, in stillness'**—through infinite time.

I am 'fullness' in my own capacity, and 'usefulness' to all facets that converge or intersect to create LIFE—through infinite time!

I am 'wisdom-compassion'—through infinite time.

I am 'vital energy in selfless service to all'—through infinite time.

I am 'infiltration and penetration of essence, primordial'—through infinite time.

LOVE, Unconditional
3

I am 'magnanimous nature, ethereal'—through infinite time.

I am 'sound and light'—through infinite time.

I am 'the convergence of past, present, and future, in this moment'—through infinite time.

I am 'myriad beings of LOVE'—through infinite time.

I am 'all wave-forms and frequencies of LIFE'—through infinite time.

I am 'the colors of change'—through infinite time.

I am 'the spectrum of radiance, effervescence, and otherwise'—from brilliance to darkness—through infinite time.

I am both 'jubilation and lamentation'—through infinite time.

I am 'the merging of joys and sorrows'—through infinite time.

LOVE, Enlightened
4

I am 'enlightened activity'—through infinite time.

I am both 'combustion and transformation'—through infinite time.

I am 'birth and evolution'—through infinite time.

I am 'preservation and propagation'—through infinite time.

I am 'dissolution and transmutation'—through infinite time.

I am 'LIFE at the crossroads'—into the 'past' and into the 'future'—through infinite time.

I am 'the ever-intersecting rivers of being' as 'name and form'—flowing—through infinite time.

LOVE, Awakened
5

I am 'the ever-changing horizon'—in space and time—through infinite time.

I am 'ceaseless phenomena'—through infinite time.

I am 'the fleeting tapestry of consciousness', called LIFE—through infinite time.

I am all 'seeds of change'—through infinite time.

I am all 'seeds of peace'—through infinite time.

I am 'the ultimate freedom of the WILL'—in all of its splendor—through infinite time!

LOVE, Virtuous
6

I am 'moral-sensitivity'—through infinite time.

I am 'freedom of the human spirit'—through infinite time.

I am 'the epitome of respect and responsibility'—through infinite time.

I am 'reverence, peacefulness, and nondiscrimination'—through infinite time.

I am 'charity, devotion, and loving kindness'—through infinite time.

LOVE, Invincible
7

I am 'humility, compassion, and sympathetic joy'—for others sake—through infinite time.

I am 'mindfulness, diligence, and patience'—through infinite time.

I am 'forbearance, vitality, and courage'—through infinite time.

I am 'self-direction, motivation, and perseverance'—through infinite time.

After all, I am 'the great seal, called mind of equanimity'—through infinite time.

LOVE, All-Pervading
8

I am 'spacious empty essence as the very ground of being'—through infinite time.

I am 'investigative, reflective attention'—through infinite time.

I am 'Nature's sublime quest as the breath of LIFE'—through infinite time.

I am 'the sentient condition'—human or otherwise—through infinite time.

LOVE, Psychedelic!
9

I am 'Nature's biorhythms'—through infinite time.

I am 'Nature's changing patterns'—through infinite time.

I am 'Nature's fulfilled nature'—through infinite time.

I am 'Nature's magnificent interdependent marvels'—through infinite time.

I am 'Nature's law and order'—through infinite time.

I am 'Nature's majesty'—through infinite time.

LOVE, All-Suffusing
10

I am 'Nature's relentless persistence'—through infinite time.

I am 'Nature's selflessness'—through infinite time.

I am 'Nature's symbiotic relationships'—through infinite time.

I am 'Nature's principles and patterns of existence and extinction'—through infinite time.

I hold 'the relative dimension'—as the space-time-continuum—through infinite time.

I am 'all expressions existential'—through infinite time.

I am 'the mysteries and marvels in existence'—through infinite time.

Nelunika Gunawardena Rajapakse

The GREAT SELF, Glorious!

Photo Credit to: Allison Scott Censori

Appreciating the Ever-Wakeful GREAT SELF

Characteristics:

Playful Wakefulness

LOVE Mirrors the Drama of Form and Being!
11

I am 'space, accommodating'—through infinite time.

I am 'celestial masses'—through infinite time.

I am 'galaxies, clusters, and super-clusters of galaxies' hurtling in space—through infinite time.

I am 'novas/novae and supernovas/supernovae', dazzling in varied intensities—through intergalactic voids—through infinite time.

I am 'stars, luminous and twinkling'—through infinite time.

I am 'comets, asteroids, and meteors' whizzing in space—through infinite time.

I am 'meteorites, as falling stars' observed—through infinite time.

I am 'planets and satellites' whirling—through infinite time.

LOVE, Wondrous!
12

I am 'momentary formations'—through infinite time.

I am 'formations, numerous'—through infinite time.

I am 'stars disintegrating'—through infinite time.

I am 'whirling dust particles and debris'—through infinite time.

I am 'the propensity to be homogeneously distributed space-particles'—through infinite time.

I am 'intergalactic space'—through infinite time.

I am 'black holes and nebulas, luminous'—through infinite time.

I am 'the universe, inconceivable and unfathomable'—through infinite time.

LOVE, Multi-faceted!
13

I am 'all aspects of perception'—through infinite time.

I am 'the electromagnetic spectrum of the universe'—through infinite time.

I am 'the waves and frequencies of cosmic vibration'—as physical, ethereal, astral, mental, emotional, psychic, and spiritual—through infinite time.

I am 'the physical properties of matter'—as light, heat, sound, electricity, magnetism, gravitation, and motion—through infinite time.

I am 'the four states of matter'—called solid, liquid, gaseous, and plasma—through infinite time.

I am 'innumerable substances'—through infinite time.

LOVE, Multi-tiered
14

Primordially, I am 'all-formations' through the interactions of four wondrous aggregate material energies—earth, water, fire, and air—through infinite time.

I am 'the unceasing combination, transformation, and redistribution' of the four aforementioned primordial material energies—through infinite time.

I am 'attractions, repulsions, and reactions' of substances—as chemistry—through infinite time.

I am 'emergent physical-frameworks', as inanimate or inorganic matter—through infinite time.

I am 'natural terrains, habitats, and adaptations'— through infinite time.

I am 'ever-emergent organisms or expressions, by natural selection', as the animate or organic world of plants and creatures—through infinite time.

LOVE, Equal and Reciprocal
15

I am 'the underlying current of evolution projecting the space-time dimension' in momentum—propelled by body, speech, and mind—through infinite time.

I am 'the balancing principle of evolution and dissolution'—through infinite time.

I am 'the substratum of LOVE eternal' bringing forth the manifestations of arising, abiding, declining, and dissolving psychophysical phenomena—along a cyclic continuum—through infinite time.

I am 'the progenitor' of the instrumental universe—for all beings of sentience—through infinite time.

I am 'the sublime moral principle of equality and reciprocity' that heals all conditions by means of interdependent causal relations—through infinite time.

LOVE, Transcendent
16

I am 'mother essence' untainted by sentient vibrations—through infinite time.

I am 'potential for diverse manifestations'—along the causal chain of psychophysical phenomena—through infinite time.

I am 'the transcendent wisdom of potent empty essence'—that surpasses the relative reality of consciousness—through infinite time.

I am 'the unifying principle that underlies all differentiations'—as modulations of omniscient awareness—through infinite time.

I am 'LOVE', unobstructed, that is the ultimate field of healing and redemption through the triple realms of matter—of desire, form, and formless existence—through infinite time.

Nelunika Gunawardena Rajapakse

The GREAT SELF
of Continuous Manifestations

Photo Credit to: Nelunika Gunawardena Rajapakse

Appreciating the Experiential Human Potential

Characteristics:

To Think, Speak, and Act

LOVE, Its Blessings!
17

I am 'diverse spiritual aspects of perception'—through infinite time.

I am 'the blessed human potential', for the sublimation of instinctual tendencies—through infinite time.

I am 'the precious human condition' serving time in the field of purposeful redemption and perfection—through infinite time.

I am 'ethnic diversity'—through infinite time.

I am 'curiosity for knowledge and wisdom'—through infinite time.

I am 'aspiration and motivation, for advancement and achievement'—through infinite time.

I am 'expression and emotion'—through infinite time.

LOVE, Its Endowments
18

I am 'attitude and its cultivation'—through infinite time.

I am 'the bearer of emotive and cognitive potential'—through infinite time.

I am 'the womb of all expressions'—from darkness to brilliance—through infinite time.

I am 'the language of LOVE'—as a spectrum of MIND—through infinite time.

I am 'the very endowment of linguistic potential'—through infinite time.

I am 'the mind of reasoning and deduction'—through infinite time.

I am 'the mind with a propensity for meticulous perfection and exactitude'—through infinite time.

LOVE, Veiled by Ignorance!
19

I am 'the past of memory'—as history—through infinite time.

I am 'history that shapes the myth of the future'—through infinite time.

I am 'the confused expression of discriminating energy'—as egocentricity—through infinite time.

I am 'the living dream'—as the mortal, corporeal condition—through infinite time.

I am 'human habitation and exploitation of my environment'—through infinite time.

I am 'the confused terrestrial wanderer seeking refuge in the perpetuation of a personal self and its attachments'—by way of sense-objects, notions, and concepts—through infinite time..

LOVE, Veiled by Discrimination and False Imagination
20

I am 'the perpetuator of deception by ignorance and discrimination'—through infinite time.

I am 'a mind-body continuum as an apparitional construct'—of mind, itself—traveling in space-time through infinite time.

I am 'a conglomeration of false imaginations sowing the seeds and reaping their harvest in terms of body-speech-mind'—along a causal continuum—through infinite time.

I am 'the master and the servant'—as the rightful heir to my acts of body, speech, and mind—through infinite time.

I am 'what I am, determined by my sole belongings'—as attachments of thought, word, and deed—through infinite time.

LOVE, Its Truth and Meaning
21

I am 'the capacity for self-realization, dispelling desire'—through infinite time.

I am innately 'the bearer of wisdom beyond reason'—through infinite time.

I am 'the experiencer of TRUTH, in conformity with MEANING', as and when the darkness of simple-minded ignorance is quelled—with zeal and purpose—through infinite time.

I am 'the great altruistic mind of the enlightened spirit'—at the service of all beings of sentience wishing for their happiness—through infinite time.

I am 'the self-realized wonder of placidity and humility'—unmoved by the psychedelic apparitional projections of terrestrial matter—through infinite time.

I am 'the sole spiritual essence, emanating the confused diffusions of form and being'—from its ever-wakeful spirit—through infinite time.

The GREAT SELF
Emanating Relative Realities

Photo Credit to: Nelunika Gunawardena Rajapakse

Appreciating the Relative Dimension

Characteristics:

Cyclic Phenomena

LOVE, as Form and Being
22

I am 'the two faces of one truth as 'the relative' and 'the absolute"—ceaselessly intertwining—through infinite time.

I am 'the inseparable union of empty essence and appearance'—flickering as 'space in time' and 'time in space'—through infinite time.

I am 'the cosmic matrix of causal relations'—as the global field of interrelatedness operating in terms of intersecting time and space—through infinite time.

I am 'the field of psychophysical phenomena, called universe'—of sensory perception—through infinite time.

LOVE, Infinite!
23

I am 'the spatial bodies' as spheres of density—from the coarsest to the subtlest levels—through infinite time.

I am 'the myriad cyclical realities', as spontaneous natural expressions spiraling in ten directions through infinite space—through infinite time.

I am 'the sun and its family'—as one, amidst other incalculable planetary systems, hurtling in space—through infinite time.

I am 'the sun's planets and satellites'—through infinite time.

I am 'Earth'—as home of terrestrial beings and forms—through infinite time.

I am 'presence alone'—as orbiting celestial bodies or masses—through infinite time.

LOVE, A Spectacle!
24

I am 'the rotations of motion'—as orbital expressions—through infinite time.

I am 'cyclic weather patterns spurred by climatic conditions'—through infinite time.

I am 'the ever-changing states of matter'—conditioned by temperature—through infinite time.

I am 'the seasons, solstices, and equinoxes'—through infinite time.

I am 'habitats, as flora and fauna, in eternal transformation'—conditioned by causes—through infinite time.

I am 'the ecological balances and symbioses'—through infinite time.

I am 'the whirling oceans and wind currents'—through infinite time.

LOVE, Limitless!
25

I am 'whatever—whenever'—through infinite time.

I am 'whenever—however'—through infinite time.

I am 'adaptation—adoption'—through infinite time.

I am 'forces and phenomena'—through infinite time.

I am 'sources and resources'—through infinite time.

I am 'concentrations and distributions'—through infinite time.

LOVE, Its Emanations!
26

I am 'blankets of density', thick to thin—to surround the planet Earth—through infinite time.

I am 'coarse Earth's tiered geosphere'—as lithosphere and barysphere (centrosphere)—through infinite time.

I am Earth's subtle-leveled density—as hydrosphere—through infinite time.

I am Earth's very subtle-leveled density—as atmosphere that encompasses the troposphere, stratosphere, mesosphere, ionosphere, and exosphere—through infinite time.

The GREAT SELF
Reflecting LIFE Spontaneously!

Photo Credit to: Nelunika Gunawardena Rajapakse

Appreciating the Magical World of Wondrous Energy!

Characteristics:

A Vibrant Energy Spectrum!

LOVE's Spectrum
of Wisdom-Compassion
27

I am 'microcosmic and macrocosmic mandalas' as interpenetrated abodes of being—through infinite time.

I am 'inseparably intertwined and interpenetrated wheels of energy (from the infinitesimal to the infinite) in rotation'—through infinite time.

I am 'energy-fields' within fields of cosmic relativity and vibration—through infinite time.

I am 'energy-fields of interdependent co-origination, in continuous manifestation'—in terms of physical, physiological, and psychological preponderance—through infinite time.

I am 'intersecting, crisscrossing, and overlapping, global fields of operation'—through infinite time.

LOVE's Expressions of the Human Spirit
28

I am 'the evolving human spirit'—through infinite time.

I am 'the expression of incessant curiosity for knowledge'—through infinite time.

I am 'the propensity for cultural aspiration'—through infinite time.

I am 'the melodies, rhythms, and diverse expressions of the spirit'—through infinite time.

I am 'the heart that emanates beauty'—as expressions of peaceful emotion—through infinite time.

I am 'dynamic or dramatic speech'—as art, music, and drama—through infinite time.

I am 'literary imagination'—through infinite time.

LOVE's Expressions of the Deeper Human Spirit
29

I am 'depth of insight as philosophy'—through infinite time.

I am 'curiosity to understand the activity of mind'—as psychology—through infinite time.

I am 'belief, faith, devotion, and wonder'—as spiritual fervor—through infinite time.

I am 'unadulterated altruistic, spiritual intention'—as wisdom and compassion—through infinite time.

I am 'desire, aspiration, and motivation towards spiritual ascent'—through infinite time.

I am 'the psychedelic spectrum of mental attitude'—from brilliance to darkness—through infinite time.

LOVE, Bestowed upon the Human Condition
30

I am 'the story of phenomena'—as existence—through infinite time.

I am 'freedom in action'—in the field of all possibilities—through infinite time.

I am 'respect and responsibility'—awaiting to give expression—through infinite time.

I am 'the energy of mindfulness'—to nurture wholesome virtues—through infinite time.

I am 'the nature and skillful means'—to expediently help overcome negative qualities—through infinite time.

I am 'the ultimate propensity to unveil the TRUTH and MEANING that underlies all vacillations of mind'—as the immutable and all-transcending 'WILL of MIND'—through infinite time.

Nelunika Gunawardena Rajapakse

The GREAT SELF of Empty Essence and Appearance!

Photo Credit to: Allison Scott Censori

Appreciating the Ultimate and Relative Dimensions of the GREAT SELF!

Characteristics:

Presence or Absence of Phenomena Based upon Causes and Conditions in the Mirror of Awareness

LOVE's Sublime Qualities!
31

I am 'truth (of empty essence) and consequences (as phenomena)'—through infinite time.

I am 'diverse effects or expressions that share the nature of their causes'—through infinite time.

I am 'aspiration for success'—so as to reap the ultimate potential, in the human condition—through infinite time.

I am 'the natural gifts of LOVE'—as charity, generosity, and integrity—through infinite time.

I am 'the pivotal attribute of stillness in dynamism'—through infinite time.

I am 'the pivotal attribute of dynamism in stillness'—through infinite time.

LOVE—The Great Seal that Contains All
32

I am 'the wonder of incessant being and becoming'—through infinite time.

I am 'the emanation of freedom in the field of infinite possibilities'—through infinite time.

I am 'the present'—as <u>all</u> expressions influenced by causes and conditions—through infinite time.

I am 'the morally ordered cosmic matrix'—of crisscrossing, overlapping, spiraling, and interweaving energy—through infinite time.

I am 'the Great Self' or 'Voidness'—supreme— spacious and unbounded with potential, beyond any or all perception, conception, and speculation— through infinite time.

I am 'the spontaneous and simultaneous interplay of one and many'—as water beneath waves, or waves upon water—through infinite time.

I am 'the union of empty essence and appearance'—
at any given moment—through infinite time.

LOVE—'Stillness in Dynamism'
33

I am Stillness in Dynamism

Every breath of life is a miracle of the moment.

It contains the universe in its entirety—untainted by thought—as infinite time.

It is devoid of representations and differentiations—as diffusions of mind.

The awakened, essential nature of mind dwells in this moment—often alluded to, within the pages of this book, as 'presence alive'.

It is the fresh breath of the moment—as awareness—in full participation with 'the here and the now'. What a marvel!

Indeed, 'this moment, of the here and the now', is the overall tapestry of being within the wholeness of one breath! This is the experience of our cosmos in its loftiest state—the ultimate attainment.

The cultivation of 'stillness in dynamism', however, is a pivotal aspect towards the appreciation and revelation of our deeper human experience of 'being engaged' in this precious moment, 'now'—as **infinite time,** in participation with the 'here'—as **infinite space.**

If this was the case, togetherness and integrity, unconditioned by thought, will be the well-depicted outcome in relation to our intrinsic awareness that permeates infinite time and space. Thus, the compassionate wisdom of unity and simplicity shall pervade the mind.

This moment, essentially, is the fullness and stillness of mind. It is the mind without vibration of thought. It is awareness of the highest order—as the immutable and all-transcendent awareness. We must treasure it with deep insight and inner composure.

LOVE—'Dynamism in Stillness'
34

I am Dynamism in Stillness

This moment is the opportunity for the 'full and useful' exercise of freedom. It is the field of pure potentiality that awaits fulfillment of benevolent action. It is the luminous, fulfilling essence of compassion—from which emerges the mortal breath of all beings and forms—that bears intrinsic importance in the field of existence, as a whole. It is the dynamic field of **the fully lived presence** in the absence of thought.

'Dynamism in stillness' and 'stillness in dynamism' are the two pivotal aspects that must be upheld with indispensable harmony, synchrony, and momentum with each other; the cultivation of these virtues calls for deeper reflection. The observation and activation of these two principles, hand in hand, help to preserve overall cosmic balance and equilibrium. It is the inherent presence that underlies both the personal and universal fields of interdependence.

Dynamism in stillness is unconditional, charitable activity that persists infinitely for the benefit of all beings—in fulfilling, interactive engagement with one another—through momentous opportunity that surges upon the OCEAN of LIFE, seen as 'UNIVERSAL MIND'.

Conversely expressed, the Tree of Life gives its precious return—by way of flowers, fruits, seeds, fresh breath, and a safe haven to those in need—when the attributes of **dynamism** in stillness have been well nurtured through every breath of 'being and becoming'.

The Universe of Myriad Inseparable Wheels in Motion
35

Infinite processes of 'being' and 'becoming' project the nature of our universal experience.

The universe, in a collective sense, is one vast and infinite, self-winding machine that embodies 'an infinity of wheels' in motion.

Despite our inability to fathom or comprehend the wondrous, vast scheme of the universe, all events by way of 'name and form, being and becoming', are inseparably interconnected wheels of energy in rotation and momentum—from the infinitesimal to the infinite.

The universe operates under two laws of conservation: of contraction and expansion.

It is an infinite phenomenon that shrinks with the infinity of contraction and expands to the infinity of extension; thus, a portion of the universe is simply a part of its infinite expanse that, in turn, contains 'an infinity' of infinitely contracted portions of the universe.

The universe may be defined as a conglomeration of an infinity of miniature universes—from the perspective of its minutest composition. Essentially, every miniscule segment contains the whole universe.

'Being and Form'

The universe of 'being and form' is our human reality. The principles that define the entirety of the universe justifiably apply to all of its parts. As such, each material fiber that constitutes 'a being' is a miniature form of the whole being, whatever might be the case.

The Universe of Flux

Of all wheels of the universe, the most powerful, inconceivable, and infinitesimally small are **the units of mind** that beat in rapidity and rotation to surpass the speed of light; similarly, **the units of matter** are movements in rotation—or wheels of energy—at a proportionately slower pace. Essentially, the mind whips matter into being; it brings forth electromagnetic sensory perceptions—as space-time objects, called matter, form, and being!

All rotations of mind and matter arise—in mutual creation; they develop, exist, decay, and dissolve—to re-evolve. This feature is a constant for both mind and matter.

Although rotations—or vibrations—consist of beginnings and endings, mind and matter are infinite phenomena without beginning or ending. They will neither cease to exist, nor remain unchanged.

Time turns every wheel of the units of mind and matter; time never remains constant; thus, no wheel of 'the units' of mind and matter shall remain constant; cycles of repetition from each beginning to ending—closely skipping from the tip of each ending to the tip of each beginning—is the order of rotational motion.

Origination leads to cessation; cessation, in turn, leads to origination. Thus, birth and death are two inevitable and interdependent, spontaneous expressions of one truth. This is the state of reality!

The universe, in essence, is a process in constant flux all over, with no uniformity of mind and matter. All units of mind, and indeed, matter discernible to the senses—only by means of substances—revolve under the universal law of continuous flux, best expressed as provisional existence.

The Tapestry of Universe
'Stillness in Dynamism' or 'Dynamism in Stillness'

Whether things or events exist near or far; visibly or invisibly; at a coarse/gross level, subtle level, or a secret essence level, all phenomena interpenetrate to form **the tapestry of the universe** bringing about revelations in relation to the law of implicate order— continually manifesting as frames of mind through each infinite moment.

The Supreme Cosmic Tapestry of LOVE—'Presence'
36

The tapestry of LOVE, of 'form and being' represents two faces of one truth; it is both selfishly personal and selflessly universal—as the paradox of life.

The tapestry of LOVE, itself, is the presence of vitality, across the universe; it is the life breath of all that is—as minerals, plants, creatures, and humans.

The tapestry of LOVE is energy that flickers as cosmic electricity pervading all phenomena of wondrous being—symbolized by the material emanations of earth, water, fire, and air—arising from, and dissolving into the potent emptiness of space.

The tapestry of LOVE deserves our invested, mindful attention; it must be nurtured personally and universally—hand in hand—with reverence.

The tapestry of LOVE is susceptible to the scars of experience—tainted by selfishness; it may be sustained with selflessness alone, since its very nature is selfless.

The tapestry of LOVE emanates many expressions; a human being is just one of many—limited in its capacity to understand the spacious, unbounded nature of Nature—as LIFE itself.

The tapestry of LOVE is simultaneously macrocosmic and microcosmic; thus, a personal human story is only a tiny aspect of a more complex and larger scheme of interrelated events.

The tapestry of LOVE calls for the continuous preservation of equilibrium among the five energies of wondrous nature—as resistance or rigidity (of earth); cohesion, adhesion, or fluidity (of water); transmutation (of fire); motion or motility (of air); and boundless infinity (of space).

The tapestry of LOVE is <u>both</u> the emanation of purity—as empty, though, potent essence—**and the field of interactivity** between the five energies that make manifest the world of discriminations and representations.

The tapestry of LOVE is the sole substance that preserves equality in all of being; it is the fundamental healing essence of wisdom-compassion—that underlies all manifestations.

The tapestry of LOVE is never the same in any two moments; it is a process of origination, evolution, preservation, transmutation, dissolution, transition, transformation, and representation—as diverse cyclic appearances comparable to flickering fireflies.

The tapestry of LOVE is analogous to the 'ocean and waves'; the waves emerge from the ocean—merging into one another—manifesting as 'waves upon water' or 'water beneath waves'.

The tapestry of LOVE awaits conditioning with respect and reverence from a personal level, since it forms an indispensable, integral aspect of its overall aura.

Hence, it is the responsibility of each individual human nature to offer its best and fullest—towards nurturing and sustaining the ever-giving and receiving tapestry of universal moral law and order.

The tapestry of LOVE is a trinity of incessant being and becoming—as essence, energy, and matter. In scientific terms, it is the revelation of the quantum soup of waves and/or particles; it is the dance of vibratory strings—as waves or filaments of energy, of which the color, flavor, and emanation are in constant flux.

The tapestry of LOVE is in relentless transience—from the coarsest to the subtlest levels of existence; phenomena, in myriad form, condition the tapestry of LOVE.

a. At the coarse level, are the material emanations or visible events in life as 'being or form'—as creatures and habitats—conditioned by physical phenomena by way of weather and climate; wind and water currents; day and night; seasons, solstices, equinoxes, eclipses, and cycles; and plants, stars, constellations, galaxies, and their orbital movements.

b. At the subtle level, is the very experience of confused and enlightened energy—such as the winds of life that ceaselessly 'evolve from' and 'dissolve into' the stillness of mirror essence.

c. At the secret level, is the wakeful experience of nature's magnanimity in the field of equanimity—wisdom and compassion—as the very substance that underlies all waveforms of 'being and becoming'.

Universe, a Chain Unbroken
37

Universe, a vast flow of events linked together in participation with one another

Universe, an unbroken chain of phenomena best described as interdependent co-origination, wherein reality as a whole is present in each of its parts

Universe, wherein things exist in relationship to others, in mutual causality

Universe, where no existence is autonomous or immutable

Universe, wherein all realities are aggregations of causes, conditions, and effects of causes by means of interdependence alone

Universe, wherein all objects of perception succumb to origination and cessation—as 'appearance and disappearance' in cyclic continuum—analogous to two blades that sharpen each other

Universe, wherein all things—from the microscopic quark, to the macroscopic galaxies—are arising, moving, evolving, subsiding, and dissolving through time and space, as gross and subtle impermanence

Universe, which is the field of infinite potential for any phenomenon to take place only because it is connected, conditioned, and in turn conditioning, co-present, and co-operating in constant transformation

Universe, wherein all conditioned things undergo change by the causes that produced them; while the causes are subject to change, all things and events that share the nature of their causes are also subject to change

Universe, wherein the cessation of continued existence of phenomena at a gross level is viewed upon as disappearance or death, while disintegration that takes place on a moment-by-moment basis is reflected upon as subtle impermanence

Universe, wherein the subtle disintegration of phenomena characterizes the various causes of events in life—thus, 'all conditioned things are impermanent'

Universe, wherein phenomena as causes and effects must accord with each other; wherein all characteristics of effects need not be present in the causal plane—though the various properties of effects must correspond to the potentialities present in the cause; wherein effects arise from the aggregation of numerous causes and cooperative conditions but not one single cause

The universe, all in all, is the playful wakefulness of wisdom-compassion, veiled and conditioned by discursive perception.

The universe, essentially, may be described as 'presence alive' surpassing body, speech, and mind!

Consciousness Inhabits a Morally Ordered Universe
38

Our universe, indeed, an unbroken continuum
A matrix—vast and supreme
Inconceivable and unfathomable
Beyond human speculation

Our universe, indeed, a consciousness continuum
Perpetuated by the 'will' of the ego
Beyond human understanding—
Of sensory perception

Our universe, indeed, of pristine moral wisdom
A reflection of subliminal checks and balances
Of cosmic order
To portray 'fruits'—as consequences
To mirror—the 'seed' acts of volition

Our universe, an autonomous field
Where ignorance, or <u>consciousness</u>—as 'seed'
Unfolds through <u>craving</u>—as 'moisture'
Thereby, the rise of the twin roots of self-
perpetuation, as aforementioned

Our universe depicts the intrinsic order
Of cosmic intelligence
Trumpeting the potential of volitional action
Blinded by delusion
Evanescent as 'fruits' of deeds
By the moral principle of interdependence

Our universe, thus, reflects the mystical aura
Of its trinity of being
As essence, energy, and matter
Of incessant becoming

Emanating vibrations
From higher to lower order
Intersecting dynamically
To bring forth consequences
Of volition—both latent and present
Ethically held accountable

Our universe, thus, in its nature of sentient being
Is conditioned, perpetuated, and regulated
By diverse orders of causation and layering
Hence, the higher to hold dominion
Over the lower orders
Of physical, biological scenes
Bending their energies in fulfillment
Of their intrinsic potential, as deemed

Our universe, though, a single matrix or tapestry—
all-embracing
As interwoven streams of consciousness
Of all living beings
These integrated fields of energy
Crisscrossing, overlapping, and merging
In fulfillment of causation and redemption
By twin roots of ignorance and craving

Our universe and consciousness—together, thus,
being self-propellant
Coexist in relationship of their mutual creation

Consciousness, the forerunner
As activity of brain-mind, or volitional stock
Steers each stream of perpetuation
From 'past to future'
Of 'being and becoming'
As seeds and fruits of actualization

Altruistic intention—as wisdom and compassion
In the wake of freedom, exercised
Through each breath of being
Leads the human condition
Onward to self-awakening

Ultimate peace
As supreme being
When 'self' is dispelled
The liberation from suffering!

The cosmic marvel of 'conditioned being and becoming' is none else but a continuous manifestation of the overall quality of psychophysical vibrations—as waves occurring upon the surface of the ocean of empty essence, that transcends all differentiations of mind.

All Things and Events Share One Substance!
39

Suchness, 'the way things are'—in this moment

Suchness, 'the supreme cosmic principle of interdependence'—as one tapestry of LOVE

Suchness, 'the luminous empty essence' that brings forth simultaneous appearance and disappearance

Suchness, 'the here' and 'the now'—as **truth and phenomena**

Suchness, 'the nature of momentary being and becoming'—as **unobstructed** truth and phenomena

Suchness, 'the unfathomable cosmos'—as the unobstructed **interpenetration** of truth (wisdom of empty essence) and phenomena (compassionate activity)

Suchness, 'the order of manifest and non-manifest being and form'—as the unobstructed interpenetration of truth **in every phenomenon**

Suchness, 'the wondrous nature of Nature'—as unrelenting freedom to be one and many at once in accordance with the law of causality

Suchness, 'sublime'—the ultimate and exquisite order transcending space and time

A Conception of the Cosmos as the Grand Scheme of Causality
40

Cosmos—a vast and inconceivable reservoir of whirling and vibrating energy fields

Cosmos—an unfathomable maze of spiraling and intercepting waves and frequencies

Cosmos—a whirlpool of forces as interfacing patterns of vibratory sound and psychedelic light

Cosmos—with neither center nor circumference, but a multidimensional energy body—as the supreme aura of light

Cosmos—a pregnant void, a matrix, a continuum of beginningless, endless whirls of oscillating energy, from the coarsest to the subtlest tiers

Cosmos—of diverse charges and their rates of vibration

Cosmos—a spectrum of transformational waves, frequencies, and patterns, the sharper or finer to penetrate the denser, by law of nature

Cosmos—of unfathomable radiance and unbounded dynamism

Cosmos—of co-existent interdependence

Cosmos—yet, the ocean in the stillness of this moment!

My Reality of 'the Here' in Space and 'the Now' in Time
41

I acknowledge the presence of all that exists—with gratitude and awareness—that my life-lessons shall continue unless and until I learn to fully unveil my primordial heart of compassion.

This moment—the present—is the omniscient TRUTH; it is all that exists. This state of mind lies between the crossroads of the past and future, when the past severs from the future.

Right here, and right now, I bow or prostrate with open arms to all of the life-conditions that continually manifest—as opportunity and circumstance—to heal me and direct me to condition my future, my destiny.

I realize that my future is upheld in the present while I may aspire to evolve in body, mind, and spirit—enabling me to remain grounded in spaciousness, as opposed to being centered upon earth.

I look upon this moment in time and space, with reverence, for I am able to stand erect due to all of the factors of interdependence—that evolved through unfolding, eternal time and, thereby, contributed to my very existence. I realize that this moment is the convergence of the past and the future—as an infinitesimally contracted portion—of the infinitely large scheme of ever-evolving time and space, called universe.

My erect body with arms stretched out in two directions exemplifies 'the present'—'the here and now'—that encompasses a vast cosmic interplay epitomizing the supreme matrix of LIFE.

When I bow to my mortal ground of being 'the Earth', I avow with gratitude to all that that has been, and all that is—right here and right now—while it continually weaves my future, my destiny!

Afterword—1

The All-Pervasive Spirit

—The Paradox of One and Many—

A Reflective Conclusion

Understanding the Tapestry of Existence

Let's Open Our Hearts to—

The Unsurpassed, Penetrating, and Perfect Scripture

The Unparalleled Supreme Cosmic Principle of Existence

—The Web of Life in this Moment!—

Afterword—1 Continued

All of name and form are infinitesimally interwoven threads of vertical and horizontal strands of space-time events. All phenomena are the adornments, or projections, at the crossroads of history and mystery. The tapestry of existence is the principle, the law, the supreme scripture, the being in momentum, the one, and the all—conditioned ceaselessly—to become reality in 'the here' and 'the now'.

It is analogous to the mythical net of 'Indra', and its precious jewels that splendidly, momentarily, and uniquely reflect their intrinsic radiance—naturally absorbed and refracted by all other jewels, without exception. This net symbolizes the 'wonder of being and becoming' conditioned in momentum by the sum quality of all other jewels that compose the net. It exemplifies the indivisible, inseparable, and interdependent nature of diverse expressions—projected as <u>one</u> unfathomable, inconceivable, universal being.

Each jewel in the net is indispensably bound by all others, and therefore, integral to the sum quality of its emanation. Metaphorically speaking, each jewel in the net exemplifies the 'personal nature' within the expansive, 'universal aspect of being and form'—together, known as 'individuality and generality'.

The personal dimension—while it is a microcosmic composition of its macrocosmic body—is limited in its capacity to view the totality of magnanimity and, as such, delusively evolves to assume 'a self' against other consciousness.

However, a cultivated vision through mindfulness should only extend the personal horizon towards the limitless, unbounded spaciousness of 'The Great Self' of selfless universal being.

This book is an exposition of the myriad and unaccountable 'Reflections in the Mirror of Mind', called 'Awareness'.

Afterword—2

Thank you, dear readers, for your time well spent to deeply understand our place in nature. We are in it together, transcending all labels and imputations of convention placed upon objects of mind.

By now, I do hope that you realize that everything is nature; and nature is the marvelous display—of the great union—of four abstract, wondrous, and infinite, material energies coalescing and dancing in space, supremely and magnanimously as multitudinous name, form, and being.

They assemble and disassemble, unceasingly, to form our world of substances. Their incessant interplay—to bring forth atomic and molecular patterns of energy—is 'the marvelous magic show' of the cosmos we know, by means of our senses, called sensory perception.

We all are witnesses to the great cosmic ballet of the substances that display the sublime energies of resistance, cohesion, transmutation, and motion infiltrated and pervaded by space—the womb of infinite possibilities!

We, together, are participants in this dance of wondrous energy—as constellations of energy, at a subtle level, or perhaps, constitutions of physical/physiological processes, at a coarse level!

From a psychological vantage point, our vibrations of energy in the great cosmic expression intrinsically possess the power and potency—both individually and collectively—to refine the dance, or even not!

Be that as it may, the deep-seated and sublime inmost force of mind—as the progenitor of higher realization—bears the essence to transform how things manifest by the energy of COMPASSION we invest upon it!

So let us be grateful for what we have, today, and return our LOVE to make our world a better place to live, each day—by the choices we make in body, speech, and mind!

About the Author

Nelunika Gunawardena Rajapakse is a proud citizen of her world having been long in residence—nearly five decades—in the United States.

She is the only daughter, besides two precious sons, of the late Dionicious and Mildred Gunawardena, who arrived in the USA, in the mid-1960's. The latter was trained directly under Dr. Maria Montessori in 1943, and it was her pride and joy to share the original version of Montessori, amidst a growing interest, then, in the United States—to assimilate and put into practice its innovative educational principles.

Nelunika, needless to say, has been a product of this unmatched authentic vision from the very inception of her life, to this day—naturally equipped to nurture, inspire, and educate, children of humanity (from birth through adolescence, and beyond), grounded in morally sensitive awareness.

About the Author—2

Mentored all along by her resolutely dedicated Montessori pedagogue mother—and, together, having worked in partnership for three decades— Nelunika is a proud beneficiary of an experientially founded, intellectual legacy. She boasts a rich, cumulative history of exemplary Montessori in practice for over forty years, having been the head directress, administrator, and chief operating officer of the much admired Bainbridge~Solon Montessori School (1970-2012) that served scores of children and parents in Ohio, USA.

The author, above and beyond all things, cherishes her morally grounded 'lived and learned' upbringing under the nurturing guidance of her parents.

About the Author—3

Nelunika's life idols, accordingly, are her parents who epitomized, through every breath of their existence, the compassionate values that remain central and universal to the great scheme called 'existence'. In observation of this view, all things, indeed, possess intrinsic richness; they call for equal value and respect—shunning egocentric norms, labels, and attitudes.

Nelunika, in turn, reflects on living a spiritually rich life through every breath of her own existence. She realizes that improvement and enrichment in sustaining values 'as a help to life'—to all that compose life—requires patience and mindful effort, hand in hand. Hence, maintaining a selfless cultivated awareness is crucial to life's overall success. The aspiration to guide others in the direction of true peace and eternal joy, thus, is Nelunika's heartfelt wish.

About the Author—4

Presently, the author lives her renewed and pioneering vision along her steadfast mission to 'Raise the Position of Today's Child and the World' while sharing her 'Vision for Intellectual Wellness for all Ages'. As such, she disseminates her wisdom and expertise through the creation of invaluable time-stamps of her life-experience.

In this day and age of confused human values and ideals, Nelunika stands passionately upon her convictions—to improve the human condition by way of books, videos, blogs, and dedicated websites.

Additionally, Nelunika Gunawardena Rajapakse is a devoted professional trainer, and a mentor for parents—engaged in sharing her expertise by way of lectures, seminars, consultations, and continuous guidance to organizations, schools, individuals, and diverse social groups.

About the Author—5

She is the author of ten books:

1. Compassionate Engaged Parenting as a Help to Life

2. Parenting as a Help to Life

3. Roots of Moral Sensitivity and the Emerging Tree of Life

4. The Active Brain—A Vision for Intellectual Wellness—Book 1

5. The Active Brain—A Vision for Intellectual Wellness—Book 2 Volume 1

6. The Active Brain—A Vision for Intellectual Wellness—Book 2 Volume 2

7. Healing Breath the Wind of Life
   (A Seeds of Wisdom Presentation—Book 1)

8. Rhythm of Nature, the Rhythm of Life!
   (A Seeds of Wisdom Presentation—Book 2)

9. Reflections Upon the Mirror of MIND (forthcoming)
   (A Seeds of Wisdom Presentation—Book 3)

10. Nature is Everything
    (A 'Seeds of Wisdom for the Maturing Intellect' Presentation for Children—Book 1)

11. Nature is Everything
    (A 'Seeds of Wisdom for the Maturing Intellect' Presentation for Children—Book 2)

Nelunika Gunawardena Rajapakse

Acknowledgement

My heartfelt gratitude goes to Debra Murray who has remained beside me to offer her gracious moral and technical support through the many pages of this book.

Nelunika Gunawardena Rajapakse

Nelunika Gunawardena Rajapakse

Nelunika Gunawardena Rajapakse